To William

Hold Fast
The Story of a Survivor

Lang Tang

Written by: Lang Tang

& Nicole Donoho

479-481-6075

8/6/24

DEDICATION

To my children and the other survivors of war.

CONTENTS

I'M A SURVIVOR

That would be the one liner I would chose to describe my life, "I'm a survivor". I have had so many near death experiences throughout my life, that I myself am often amazed to still be alive and well. Some people have known me as Phang and others have known me as Phang Mean. My real name is Lang Tang.

In the country of Cambodia, from 1975 to 1979, an estimated 2.5 million people died. Some of them from disease, some of from starvation, and others brutally murdered by the Khmer Rouge regime. Overtime, these mass graves have come to be known as the Killing Fields.

To most people, the victims of the events surrounding the Killing Fields are just nameless faces in documentaries and collected stories. To me, these victims had dreams and hopes beyond their short lives. They had names and families. They had struggles and hardships. They had lives I can relate to because I have walked where they walked. I am a survivor of the Killing Fields.

There were so many moments in my life I thought that I might die, and there were others I begged for it. And yet here I am, alive and well. All it takes for a person to remain nameless is for one man to remain quiet. This is my time to talk. This is my time to share.

If I'm writing this only for a history lesson, then so be it. But perhaps, just maybe, there is a greater purpose in this story. It may find someone who is confined in bondage. It might cross paths with a lonely person on their last thread of hope. It may reach someone who is about to give up.

If you find this to be you, may you know and understand, above all else, that often times the mind is our greatest prison. May you know that there is always hope until the last breath you breathe, just so long as you are willing to search it out and hold tight to it. And may these truths find you and comfort you in your darkest of hours when the light seems to be moments from fading.

My name is Lang Tang and this is my story.

*"Then you will know the truth,
and the truth will set you free."
John 8:32*

Lang Tang & Nicole Donoho

A SEARCH FOR SOMETHING MORE

January 1, 1951 is where my story begins. I was born in the city of Travinh located in South Vietnam. Although, I was born in Vietnam my true heritage is Cambodian.

At one time, this portion of Vietnam was owned by the country of Cambodia. Through a series of events, France took ownership of this land and then gave it to Vietnam. Cambodians are still fighting to this day for this portion of their land to be returned to their country.

I was the third child born in my family, altogether there were ten children. We were a very poor family. For that reason, my older brother and sister were required to work in the rice fields with my parents.

When I turned six years old, my parents decided to take me to school so I could learn the Vietnamese language. There was a lot of fighting going on in Vietnam during this time. Walking to school was often like taking a stroll through a battlefield. We could never be sure what might happen. Sometimes they would bury landmines on roads in attempts to destroy military vehicles. However, these landmines were usually more likely to destroy civilian vehicles instead- city buses, motorcycles, and other unsuspecting victims. Some days we would have to leave school early because fighting would break out and other days they would warn us before the school hours so we would not even attend school that day.

I continued school until the sixth grade. At that time, I was fourteen years old and I found myself wanting something more than what I'd lived. I told my parents that I would like to read and write in my native tongue, Cambodian. I asked them if they would allow me to attend school in Cambodia. At fourteen, I had seen many people escape from Vietnam to Cambodia. Most of these people went on to have very successful careers in life after attending the Cambodian schools. I myself had big dreams as well. Dreams that did not seem like they could become a reality unless I began to pursue them as soon as possible. My parents asked me what I wanted to do with my life. I told them that I wanted to be a pilot. What a great job that would be to fly people around in those huge planes! My parents agreed that it was a great career choice. They also agreed that in order for me to achieve such dreams, I would have to attend school in Cambodia.

At that time, crossing the border between Vietnam and Cambodia was very dangerous because of division and war within the country of Vietnam. The Vietnamese government didn't want anyone leaving the country, especially those with Cambodian heritage like me. They knew that most people would not return once they left.

Even though my parents knew this trip would benefit me, it was not something they wanted their fourteen year old venturing off alone on. From my house to the border was a whole day's ride if you went by motorcycle. Thankfully, my uncle had a dream of furthering his education as well. He understood how important this was to me. He agreed to take me across the border and find me a safe place to stay. He wouldn't be able to stay with me though because he was a monk. He would have to return to the Cambodian temple in Vietnam once I was safe.

We reached the border and began looking for someone that would help us cross the border. Because it was so dangerous we'd have to find someone with experience if we wanted to safely make the journey.

We found someone and were soon given instructions:
"You must be quiet."
"You cannot look back."
"You cannot stop no matter what!"
And finally, "When you see the Cambodian soldiers run to them as fast as you can because they will help you."

We stayed near the border that night and around 4:30 in the morning my uncle and I, as well as a small group of others, boarded a fishing boat to cross the border by the river. Once we reached the shore, we began to run through the woods. The woods smelt so bad. I asked the man what the horrible smell was but he told me to be quiet and keep running.

I later found out that the smell had come from decaying bodies. The bodies of those that had tried to cross the border weeks or even just days before us. They had not made it and their bodies were left as warnings to others that might attempt such acts.

We were about two hundred yards to Cambodian land when gunfire broke out behind us. The soldiers yelled at us to stop immediately as they continued to fire at us. The soldiers wanted to scare us to come back but they weren't actually allowed to shoot people on Cambodian land, so they would shoot up in the air. It didn't matter what direction they were shooting it still frightened us.

The man leading our group yelled at us, "Keep running and don't stop". Cambodian soldiers began to run towards us and then past us. Other Cambodian soldiers waved us in to safe areas. The soldiers asked if anyone was hurt or left behind. My uncle and I said no. We weren't thinking about anyone else in the group, just each other. We were both alive, we were both safe, and that's all that mattered to us.

They took us into their camp. We stayed there for four days answering questions and waiting for our paperwork to be processed. Since we were of Cambodian heritage they gladly accepted us into the country, no passports or visas required. They would ask people if they had family living in Cambodia and what city you would like to go to. If you didn't have any family in the country, the Cambodian government would take care of you. They would provide a house, a farm, and some animals for you to start your life in Cambodia. They never limited how long they supported you, they just wanted to be sure that you could provide for your family before they left you on your own.

Once everything was settled we got on a bus and went to Phnom Penh, the capitol of Cambodia. We stayed there for one night and went on to Kratie. Fifteen, maybe even as much as twenty, years ago people from my village in Vietnam escaped and began new lives in Kratie. Some of the people of Kratie still remembered my parents and my uncle.

My uncle spoke with a couple in the village and asked if they could take care of me. He would have to return to Vietnam but he wanted to make sure that I could stay and work with them once he left. He also wanted to make sure that they would send me to school. They agreed that they would do this for my uncle, so he returned to Vietnam leaving me in their care.

Shortly after my uncle's departure I began to question the couple about when I would begin attending school. I had crossed the border and I was in Cambodia. Something I had previously dreamed about. I was ready to attend school immediately. They told me that school had all ready started some time before I had arrived. I would need to wait until the next school year began before I could plan on attending.

While waiting for the next school year to arrive I began working on their farm. When the next school finally arrived I approached the couple again. This time they told me that I was too old to attend school. I became like a slave to them. They had me working long hours, from early in the morning until dark. I was tired and lost a lot of weight during that time. I remember crying a lot because I felt as if there was no hope for me.

Although I did not know God at that time I know that He must have been looking out for me. I remember one of the days on the farm I was cutting down weeds with three men. We used long handled knives with long straight blades, similar to machetes. One of the men accidentally threw his knife in the air. The blade came down on my head. Blood was gushing from my head and I thought it must be really bad.

"How deep is it?" I asked.

He must have been really nervous because he spread his fingers about two inches. "No, how deep is it?" I asked again, realizing that he was showing me how long it was. They never took me to the doctor. The couple put some medicine on it and I continued to work. I still have that scar to this day.

Despite the despair I felt, I managed to muster up the courage to speak with the couple once again and plead my case. I told them that my goal had been to come to Cambodian and attend school. If I was going to work all day long I would be better off returning to Vietnam. They told me that I could not go home by myself.

I cried. I wanted to go home so badly but they threatened to call the police if I tried to leave. "Your uncle told us to watch you. We agreed to this so we cannot let you leave alone." They told me. I'm not sure if God changed their heart at that moment but they soon gave me another option. If I could find an adult to go with me, they would let me go home.

I asked everyone in the village if they would be willing to take me home to my parents. No one wanted to return to Vietnam. While the trip into Vietnam was no problem, they knew that getting back to Cambodia would be very difficult. The Vietnamese gladly opened their borders to receive people, it was the leaving part that they seemed to have problems with.

After almost giving up hope, I came across an old woman. She had lived in my village back in Vietnam not far from my house. I spoke with her and told her my story. She told me that she would gladly take me home but she would have to save up money first. I worked for three more months, that felt like the longest three months ever. She finally had the money saved and we took a bus to Vietnam.

When I arrived at my home, my parents cried because they didn't even recognize me at first. In the year that I had been gone, I had lost so much weight and my skin had darkened a lot from working in the fields. I had never worked that hard before in my life. My mom cried, she didn't want me to leave ever again. They both agreed that I should stay home from now on.

Even though I was glad to be away from the hard work and be back home with my family, I knew in my heart that I still had a dream. I still had the desire to read and write in the Cambodian language. And it wasn't a dream that I wanted to let die. I decided to do whatever I could where I was so I moved in to the Cambodian temple in Vietnam. I lived there for a year before becoming a Cambodian monk.

Not only would it allow me to learn the Cambodian language but it would also keep me from being recruited into the army. I had no desire to join the war so it seemed like the best option all together.

Many people in Vietnam died during this time because of the big war between America and Vietcong. I have heard the death tolls were somewhere in the tens of thousands. I thank God that I had become a monk and was able to stay away from the war. It was January 30, 1968, the Chinese New Year, and I was seventeen years old. I finished my second year of school in the Cambodian language. I could now read and write Cambodian very well but I still had the same dream. I wanted to return to Cambodia and become more successful.

I told my parents that this dream had not left me. I would like to return to Cambodia once more. Although they did not want to see me leave they agreed that this would once again be the best path for me. It would allow me to further the education I had started at the temple.

My uncle, the one who had volunteered to take me the first time, volunteered to go with me once again. He too still had a dream. He was also a monk and wanted to further his education to be a scholar. This time he planned on staying with me once we got to Cambodia. So once again we made the trip back to the border.

BACK TO CAMBODIA

At three o' clock in the morning, we crossed the river by fishing boat. I remembered the horrible smells from our first experience of crossing the border three years before. This time was no different. This time we could see human bones all over the banks of the river as we exited the fishing boats and the smell of the decaying bodies was so strong.

It was very quiet. We walked through the woods without any problems and soon arrived at the Cambodian camp. We stayed there for a few days before going on to Phnom Penh.

During that time, Cambodia had just begun a civil war. Khmer Rouge regimes were rising up as part of the communist parties in Cambodia. Because the Khmer Rouge were a branch off of the Vietnam People's Army of North Vietnam, the Cambodian government suspected anyone that acted differently or did not join in their government to be part of the Khmer Rouge regime. For this reason, monks were among their first suspects.

The lifestyle of a monk was rather simple. Monks were only allowed to eat from sunrise until noon during the day. Since we did not have jobs, we would go through the village and collect food from the villagers. Most of the villagers would participate in contributing to the monks. They would give small portions of food to each monk, maybe a small piece of fish from one house or a small spoonful of rice from another.

My uncle and I had been living as monks in Phnom Penh for almost six months. One day, the Cambodian police approached my uncle and told him that he could no longer leave the temple. Nothing good could come from him being confined to the temple. He would no longer be able to collect food to eat each day.

He knew that the police suspected him to be involved with the Khmer Rouge and would soon arrest him. He told me that I must leave the temple immediately before they arrest me as well. I fled to the Sadao temple in the city of Campong Cham. There I met other Cambodian monks that were born in Vietnam like me. I stayed at the temple that whole next year and continued my schooling. I never heard back from my uncle and wouldn't hear from him again until 1985.

Because we were Cambodians born in Vietnam, we seemed to remain stuck in the middle of everything. The Cambodian government suspected us to be involved with the Khmer Rouge which often lead to imprisonment. The Khmer Rouge suspected we were involved with the Cambodian government which often lead to imprisonment or even death. The temple seemed to be one of the safer places, but not always as I soon found out.

A fellow monk returned one night and warned me and the other monks from Vietnam, "You must leave immediately. I have overheard the police talking about arresting all of you. They suspect you're involved with the Khmer Rouge. If you stay until morning, you will surely be arrested."

I left immediately on a boat to the city of Kratie. This was the same city my uncle took me to when I was fourteen. I knew people in the village and asked them where I might find the nearest temple to continue with my education. Although life was crazy with the war, continuing my education was still the top priority in my mind. One of the families in the city told me that I needed to go to the Sambo temple to continue my education. I went to the Sambo temple and studied for another year.

In 1970, the United States government stepped in to help the Cambodian government take a stand against the Khmer Rouge. They overthrew Sihanuk, the Cambodian king, because he reported to China. Once he was overthrown, he returned to China and gave an account of what was happening. During this time, five cities fell under Khmer Rouge rule- Kratie, Stungtreng, Ratanakiri, Mondolkiri, and Pravihear. During the next three years nothing drastic happened but that soon changed.

"To keep you is no benefit,
To destroy you is no loss."

-the motto of the Khmer Rouge

THE KHMER ROUGE RULE

In 1973, Pol Pot, the Khmer Rouge leader, told villagers they were no longer allowed to feed the monks. Without the handouts from the people, the monks were forced to leave their temples and lifestyles behind. The Khmer Rouge forced the monks to remove their robes and dress in regular clothing, stripping them of their identity. After that they forced the monks to work for them. Praying and studying was no longer an option for the monks. There were no more monks during that time because of these events.

The Khmer Rouge took us to a small village and forced us to work in the rice fields. We lived in the jungle during that time. Many people were dying from the living conditions and hard work. One of the rules the Khmer Rouge forced us to live by was "no work, no food". It was simple, if we did not work then we would not eat. Not that they fed us very much to begin with.

If we were sick and could not work then we did not eat either. It was during this time that I became ill with malaria. Once again, God must have been looking out for me during those six long months. Sometimes I would be given some food and sometimes I'd go long periods without any. The Khmer Rouge soldiers left me lay there to die. I was down to skin and bones before I began to recover.

After I my near death experience with malaria, I had another experience that almost claimed my life. I was given instructions to go hunting one night. Back then, we didn't have small flashlights with batteries. We had lights with large battery packs attached to them. These packs weighted thirty, maybe forty, pounds and it was my job to walk behind the hunter carrying the heavy pack attached to his light. I couldn't see very well since the light was in front of me which caused me to step on a poisonous snake.

The snake bite my foot and I was in so much pain. I couldn't sleep at all that night. I cried because it hurt so much. I wasn't sure what to do and neither was anyone else. Once again, the Khmer Rouge thought it would be best to leave me there to die. One less mouth to feed.

The next morning, one whole side of my body from head to toe was swollen black and blue. An old man came to me, I was told he was some kind of witch doctor or something like that. He told me that he knew what kind of medicine would heal me. He fed me some medicine and put something on my head. The swelling went down and my skin began to go back to normal within a couple of hours. I don't know what he did but it saved my life.

While I was living with the Khmer Rouge, we'd have nightly meetings. They would ask us question after question to find out more about us. I soon realized that lying was the only way I might make it through these meetings alive. They asked what kind of education we had. The ones that had educations and were known as teachers or scholars were often killed. They asked where we were from. If you were from Vietnam, you would be killed. When they questioned me I told them my name was Phang (pronounced pounge) it was my brother's name and it was Cambodian. I told them I was born in the Cambodian city of Battambang, I was an only child, and my parents were both dead. This kept them from investigating about my family which they often did to others. I also told them I was a monk and I had no education. Because I spoke Cambodian so well, they believed me.

During that time, B-52 bombers would pass over Cambodia and drop bombs wherever they suspected Vietcong soldiers to be stationed. One day a bomb was dropped less than a mile from the place I was living. The Cambodian homes are built up on stilts so they stand about two stories off the ground, similar to houses built in Louisiana in the United States, but they don't have any walls. When the bomb hit, I fell from the house. My ears were ringing and my back was sore. This pain stayed with me for most of my life causing me to walk like an old man but I'll come back to that later.

There was so much war in the country at that time. Bombs were going off within the country and gunfire was everywhere. From 1975-1979, Cambodians referred to this as year zero. There was no money. There was no market. There were many people that threw away their gold and silver at that time because it had no value to them. They were only concerned about food to eat so they could survive.

In 1975, Khmer Rouge cleared the remainder of the monks from every temple in Cambodia. They converted most of the empty temples into military bases that stored food, supplies, or prisoners. The Khmer Rouge gained a victory against the American allies in April of that year.

This is the year I also became a truck driver for the Khmer Rouge. Whatever job the Khmer Rouge gave you, you had to take and not complain about it. If you complained, they told you that you had to move. When they told you this it meant that you would soon be killed.

I hauled any supply that they needed from village to village. I was expected to take excellent care of the vehicles I operated because if something went wrong I would be suspected of tampering with the vehicle. Tampering with the vehicle could possibly result in death. The Khmer Rouge had little value for life. They would kill people that spoke against them. But the list didn't stop there. Have a friend in the American military? You'll be killed. Have an education? You'll be killed. It seemed like they might even kill you just for looking at them the wrong way or breathing wrong. The best thing to do was keep your head down, keep your mouth shut, and work hard at whatever task you were given.

One night, it was storming very hard. My truck stalled on top of a hill. When I got out to use the hand crank and restart it, I got struck by lightning. After getting struck, I fell to the ground and my truck ran over me, rolled down the hill and hit a tree. I didn't get in trouble though because I regained consciousness and got up. They never found out about it.

I remember a man that was a friend of mine. The Khmer Rouge found out that he had family associated with the US military. They arrested him. He escaped, as he was running away they shot at him. They couldn't find him for two days and so they thought he was dead. But I found out later that he crawled back to the camp. He went to the kitchen tent and begged the cook to give him some food. The cook refused because he knew the Khmer Rouge would kill him just for helping. He left to get the soldiers and the man ate what he could while the cook was gone. He knew it would be his last meal. The soldiers came to the tent and no one heard from my friend again.

The supply convoys that I drove on would usually send ten trucks out at a time. Most of the time they would send extra people on these convoys. I soon began to realize that these people were ones that had been labeled enemies of the Khmer Rouge. Halfway through the trip we would stop and these people would be called into a tent or even just on the side of the road where they would execute them. I had many friends that died. But as I said before, to stay alive you must be blind, deaf, and dumb. Asking questions about where someone was or what had happened to them would only get you killed as well.

I drove my truck and kept it running well. Although I still did not know God at this time, He allowed me to gain favor among my enemies through my hard work. In 1977, the soldiers in charge of me decided I was trustworthy. They liked my attitude and dependability so they recommended me to become a driver for one of the Khmer Rouge commanders. This man told me that I should no longer worry about anyone killing me because he was in charge and I worked for him. Not too long after that, Pol Pot's soldiers killed him and his family. This was not uncommon for the Khmer Rouge to kill people in their own ranks. Life meant nothing to them. They killed whomever they wanted, whenever they felt like it. This put me out of work and of course in fear of my life again. I no longer had protection.

Shorty after they killed the commander they began to investigate me because of my job as his driver. They asked me many questions but I never told them anything. They thought that I might be involved with him but eventually dropped the investigation.

In January 1978, I married my first wife. On September 16, 1978 my first daughter, Sophoeun Phang, was born. They told me she was very special because she had a veiled birth. My wife's water had not broke and my daughter came out still inside of the protective ammoniac bubble. The midwife had to cut her out after delivery. Around this same time, Vietnam invaded Cambodia and the Khmer Rouge forced all the people to go with them.

THE DEADLY JUNGLE JOURNEY

The eight months we spent wandering through the jungle were very difficult. We ate whatever we could find- fruit, snakes, bugs- just to survive. Many people died every day, especially young children. The babies that were breast feeding were the first to die because their mothers had nothing to feed them. My daughter was only about three months old when we entered the jungle. In our group, my daughter and another boy were the only little ones that I remember surviving. Babies would cry so much because of the lack of food until they would finally stop crying. At that point it wasn't long before they would die.

It was also difficult for pregnant women at that time. One woman, my friend's wife, fainted and laid on the ground unconscious. She was probably eight months pregnant. The Khmer Rouge told my friend, "The Vietnamese soldiers are very close. We have to keep moving. We have to keep moving."

Since we didn't have time for any type of proper burial we covered her with whatever we could find, leaves and branches, and went on. She was still alive but there was nothing we could do for her. Three or four hours later we were forced to return to the same area. My friend searched everywhere for his wife's body but it was gone. Most likely, it had been drug away by a tiger. Words cannot truly explain the pain and agony my friend went through at that moment. He cried and cried over the loss of his wife and unborn child, knowing that he had to bury them alive.

There are others that I remember as well. Some mothers screamed during labor and delivery "Please someone help me". but no one in the group would stop to help them. The Khmer Rouge forced us to continue moving. They told women carrying small babies that they should leave the crying babies or leave the group and stay with their babies. Either choice led to death. Carrying a crying baby meant that enemy soldiers could easily find us. Staying with a crying babies meant you were alone and would be killed by soldiers or wild animals.

One woman had a small baby about my daughter's age. The baby cried and cried all the time. One day we no longer heard the baby crying and no one thought anything of it. About two or three years later, after we had met her again in America, we found out that she had thrown her baby into the river that night back in the jungle. She said she lived with the nightmare from that moment on. Even though years had passed she could still hear her baby's cries at times.

The Khmer Rouge kept us with them as their human shields. They forced us to walk in front of them. When they came across enemies they would open fire. The enemies would return their fire, killing off many of the human shields. Many people died because we were unarmed. There was no safety for us. The Khmer Rouge would kill you if you tried to leave the group. Even if someone did attempt to leave, it was very dangerous. Tigers roamed the jungle and were ready to attack anyone that strayed too far from the others.

I remember them bringing rice to the soldiers. I begged them to give me some rice for my family. They refused. I'm not proud of what I did but I did what had to be done to keep my family alive. One night, while the soldiers were sleeping, I snuck over to them and stole a bag of rice. It was enough to feed my family for a few weeks. That same night I cooked the rice at about one or two o' clock in the morning so no one would know what I had done. We were so happy to have food.

The jungle was such a hard place to live. It was full of so much death. There was a night guns began firing and so we ran. We ran hard to get away. That night we came across a pond. Everyone in the group was so happy. We didn't often get very much water to drink, if any at all. We were so thirsty and so we began to drink some water.

The next morning when we woke up we saw that the pond was full of dead bodies. The bodies of the group that was just ahead of us. We realized then that it was a trap. Renegade thieves would wait for people to approach the water for a drink and open fire on them. They weren't for Khmer Rouge, they weren't for Cambodia, they simply killed to get whatever they could from whomever crossed their path. During that time, we soon realized any place that had water would also have dead bodies.

JUST OUTSIDE OF THAILAND

We arrived at the Thai border and everybody that survived set up tents just outside the border. My body was very swollen and I became very sick because of the lack of food. I thought for sure I would die. This had become a common thought and I was almost use to the reality of it now. I told my family goodbye and I walked down to the river. I hoped that I might find some fish in the river but I couldn't find any fish.

Once again, God had his eye on me. While I was standing there, ready to die, a large bird, some kind of goose, flew over my head and landed in the water in front of me. I grabbed a stick and immediately killed the bird. I was so happy I could hardly believe this had happened for me.

I took the bird back to my tent so my family could eat. We even had enough to share with my friend and his family as well as leftovers for the next day. It felt so good to have food in my stomach once again.

Some of the people in our group had gold, silver, or bronze. They would take these things to the Thai people and buy lots of food for their families. I didn't have any of these things. I was very hungry and decided to ask if they might share some of their food but they said that they could not. Nobody cared about each other, we were at war. Their only concern was to survive to the next day. Who knows what might happen beyond that.

I noticed some people killing a cow in a nearby tent. I went to them and asked if they could spare a little meat for me and my family.

"No, this is for our family to eat." They told me.

"Could you not even spare some of the skin?" I begged.

"No, we can't give you anything." They replied.

"You people are very mean!" I yelled angrily. How could they be so selfish with so much food that they could not even spare a small piece, not even the skin? They moved away from the camp after that. I walked over to that area to see if there was anything left to eat but it was all rotten and could not be eaten.

There was a day that I decided to cross the river and head to the Thai marketplace hoping that I might find someone generous enough to spare some food. On my way, I found a bronze pot. It was probably only worth one or two dollars but it would be enough to buy me some food. I was very happy to find it.

Some Khmer Rouge soldiers found me with the pot and took it away from me. They told me that I should not sell my pot. Selling it to the Thai people would just be wrong, it would make the Khmer Rouge look bad. I told them I was very hungry and had not eaten in a lot of days. They had mountains of rice stored up for the soldiers, could they not spare some of that food for me to eat then.

"No, that food is for the soldiers." They objected. I all ready knew that we were not allowed to touch it. Even the food that they threw away could not be touched because it often spoiled too quickly to be eaten.

I met a lady later that day that had purchased twenty five pounds of rice. I offered to carry it to her tent and she gladly accepted. I had hoped that she might give me some of the rice she had purchased but when we arrived to her tent she did not.

I laid in my tent and decided that the only way I would live, would be to go and work for the Thai people. Every day people would cross the border looking for work so they could get food but they would be killed. On my way to cross the border, the Khmer Rouge stopped me and asked where I was going. I told them that I would like to go to Thailand to find food to eat. The soldier told me that Angka, the leaders of the Khmer Rouge, would take care of their people. I shouldn't go to Thailand for food. I informed him that I had not eaten in eight days. My body was once again swollen.

"I'm going whether you give me permission or not!" I told the soldiers. I was hungry and I had to get something to eat.

One of the soldiers drew a line in the dirt. "If you cross this line, I will shoot you."

Even though I often felt as if I was on death's doorstep, I still didn't have an actual desire to die. I regretfully retreated to my tent. But I would not give up. "It's time to leave." I told my wife when I returned to the tent.

My daughter was about ten or eleven months old at that time. She was very small and she would only open her eyes a very little bit. She wouldn't usually cry because she didn't have any energy to but she was still alive. We told my friend and his wife that we were leaving. They grabbed their baby and the six of us went into the jungle together.

Even though the jungle would be full of scorpions, snakes, and spiders- those were the least of our concern. If we saw any of them they might scare us but they could easily be killed or gotten away from. What concerned us more was the chance that we might stumble across a buried landmine or worse sharpened bamboo stuck into the ground. Since most people, except soldiers, walked around barefoot a painful way to discourage people from wandering where you didn't want them to was to sharpen bamboo like twelve inches spears and push them into the ground. That way it would go through your foot when you stepped on it. They would also bury landmines around the areas of sharpened bamboo just in case people thought about walking around them.

They often had the people they were holding captive sharpen the bamboo for them. I believe this helped to instill a fear in the people so they would chose not to escape.

We walked through the jungle for six hours. Up and down the mountain. We fell many times, got back up, and continued on. We would listen for the vehicles on the nearby road to determine that we were going in the right direction. We heard the loud shots from machine guns many times but continued to press on through the jungle.

We reached a cornfield of a farmer that lived just outside the jungle. We began to eat corn right off the stalks. We were so hungry. My friend spoke Laos, which is very similar to Thai, so he went up to the farmer's house. His wife stayed in the cornfield with me and my wife just to make sure it was safe.

The farmer talked with my friend. He knew that he was Cambodian or Vietnamese and would work for food and shelter. He asked my friend how many people were with him. He told the farmer there were four adults and two babies. The farmer told him that we all needed to get into the house quickly because the Thai soldiers might kill us if they saw us wandering around.

FINDING REFUGE IN THAILAND

We had plenty of food to eat while we were living there. The landlord loved us very much because we were hard workers. We were just glad to have food and shelter once again. The landlord told us that he wanted to help us become Thai citizens. He was going to give us some land and help us get started. We lied to him and told him that sounded like a good plan, but really we were only interested in getting food. I stayed with the landlord almost three months before moving on but during that three months there were many things that happened.

Every night the Khmer Rouge brought gold, silver, and other things to sell to the Thai soldiers. I was so scared that one day they might recognize me and send me back to Cambodia or even kill me. Then it got worse, they began asking my landlord for work to make money. My landlord put me and my friend in charge of overseeing the workers. He told us that our only job now was to make sure the other workers were doing their jobs.

I covered my face so that they could not recognize who I was. I'm glad that I did because one day the soldier that had drawn the line in the sand came to work. I knew if the soldier recognized me, he would kill me. I also knew that if I told the landlord who he was and how he had threatened me, the landlord would kill him. I decided it was best to keep my mouth shut.

Finally, one day, a soldier recognized me and remembered who I was. He told the others and they said that they would soon kill me. My landlord found out about the threat and told us that we needed to leave immediately. It was no longer safe for us to live with him. He had a cousin that lived further into Thailand, deep within the jungle. He knew that we would be safe there so he sent us to stay with his cousin.

Both of our families lived with his cousin for six months. They loved us very much just the same as our first landlord. We slept well, we ate well, and again he told us that we should stay with him and become Thai citizens. "Don't return to Cambodia." He warned us. We agreed with him but knew in our hearts that we wanted to eventually return to Cambodia.

On January 17 1979, the Vietnam soldiers chased Khmer Rouge out of Cambodia. The Khmer Rouge fled to Thailand, discarded their weapons and uniforms, and hid in the refugee camps among the other people. The UN workers would leave the camp at night and return during the day to make sure there was food for the refugees. While they were gone, Khmer Rouge would hold secret meetings every night in the refugee camp trying to recruit people to return and fight Vietcong.

One day, my friend asked me if we wanted to live in the refugee camp. "What will happen when we go to these camps?" I asked.

"You don't have to work at these camps, they just give you food for free." He said, "And if you go to these camps you will have a chance to go to the third country."

"What is the third country?" I asked. It was not something I had heard of before.

"America." He smiled and told me, "In America, people live free. Not like how they live in our countries."

I heard that and really liked the idea of being free. We got our families and decided to leave. The landlord's son cried and begged us to stay until his father got home. He was the only one home at the time. I told him that we were very sorry but we had to leave right away. I knew that there would be no chance of leaving when his father got home. He would make us stay with him if he found out that we were planning to leave.

I later found out that the boy's parents came to the refugee camp looking for me. If they had found me at the camp they would have had the Thai soldiers arrest me and take me back to their farm. They probably would have told them that I worked for them and ran away or something in that nature. Thankfully, I had all ready left the camp before this happened.

UNHCR, United Nations High Commissioner for Refugees, provided food for people living in the refugee camps. It sounded like this free food was a great thing. However, most of the people came to the camps starving. Their bodies were so deprived of food that when they ate their bodies couldn't handle it. They ate so much food so fast that many of them died.

I was given the job of maintaining the machine that pumped water for the camp. My family and I were ok living at the camp. Every day people would ask me when I planned on returning to fight Vietnam in Cambodia. I told them they should go first because I wasn't ready yet. The truth was that I had no desire to join the war. Thai soldiers would help take care of the camps to ensure the refugees safety. They found out that I spoke Thai so they would often ask me if I knew of any Khmer Rouge staying in the camp.

Most of the Khmer Rouge soldiers would hide in the camp to take advantage of the free food being distributed. They would come and go taking food to the other soldiers. I knew them all but I never told the Thai soldiers what I knew. Rule number one at the temple was that monks were never to kill. I suppose that rule stuck with me because even though I came across many Khmer Rouge that had mistreated me, I did not want to see anyone die. Especially not because of me.

The Khmer Rouge would come to me and ask me when I was planning on returning to Cambodia. They wanted me to come with them and fight. If I told them I would not ever return with them they would find a way to kill me as they had done to others. So instead, I told them that I could not go with them yet. I had to take care of the pump for the camp. It would not be good for me to leave yet.

THE FAVOR OF GOD

In 1980, a woman that I had met during the escape from Cambodia, came to me at the refugee camp and asked me to write letters to her brother. Nobody in their family could read or write at all. She asked me about my parents and family and I told her the truth. It had been a long time since I told anyone the truth about my family and where I had come from. She took me on as an adopted son. I began to call her my godmother.

Her brother was allied with the United States army during the war. When the Khmer Rouge took over Cambodia the US army helped their allied escape to Thailand and shortly after sent them to America. Her brother sent her money. She asked for me and my family to stay with her and offered to help take care of us. She was so nice to my family. She treated me like one of her sons. Up until this point, I did not have a last name. I was only known as Phang which was not uncommon back then. When I had to have a last name I took on her husband's last name Mean, and became Phang Mean. That is the name everyone knew me by until I became a US citizen in 1989. When I became a US citizen I could once again use my real name, Lang Tang.

Her brother began writing letters every month. He told us that we should not go back to Cambodia. He told us that we should give up our religion and become Christians. Then come to America. He knew the religion we had, he had once believed in it and practiced it as well. "But I now realize Jesus is real and I choose to serve him." He told us in his letters.

Around this time, my second child was four or five weeks from being due. In Cambodia, the mothers would begin drinking a small glass of sesame seed and wine mixture on a daily basis during their last weeks of pregnancy. They didn't have a lot of medicine and this mixture often helped to ease the labor pains.

I didn't have any money to buy the supplies needed so every day when I got beans to eat I would set some aside until I had enough to sell. The Thai people waited outside the refugee camps for people to come out and sell stuff to them. When I had enough saved up I decided to go see the Thai people. When I did this, a Thai soldier saw that I was trying to sell things to the Thai people and arrested me.

I thought for sure my life would end at this moment. Thai soldiers were known for treating their prisoners just awful especially Cambodian people. They made me sit on the ground at the camp in the exposed sun. It beat down on me and made me sweat so bad. It was so hot out. I finally decided to close my eyes and talk to this new God I decided to follow. "I don't know who Christ is but I know I gave my life to him a week ago so maybe God can help me now."

Right after I prayed that, one of the Thai commanders yelled at me in Thai. He said to come over by him and I responded in Thai. He was surprised and the tone in his voice immediately changed.

"Where did you learn to speak Thai?" he asked me.

"I lived with a Thai family. I worked for them and they provided me with food and shelter after escaping from the Khmer Rouge." I replied, "They taught me to speak Thai."

"Why have you gotten in trouble?"

"My wife is pregnant. I was trying to sell some beans so that I could buy her the medicine she needs for when the baby arrives."

"Why didn't you come to me and tell me this to begin with?" He asked.

"I didn't know that I could do this." I replied.

"What do you do at the refugee camp?"

"I maintain the water pump to make sure there is water in the camp."

The commander thought for a moment and then looked at me. "Do you know how to cook?"

"Yes."

"You should stay here and cook for my soldiers." He replied, "I will give you everything that you need to take care of your wife and you won't have to sell stuff anymore."

I stayed with the Thai soldiers and cooked for them. A few days went by and my godmother stopped at the gate insisting to talk with the commander. She was worried that I had been injured or killed. He told her that I was ok but I could not leave just yet. I had work to do.

During that month, I took care of everything that I was asked to do. I cooked, I cleaned, I washed soldiers laundry. Whatever job was asked of me, I would do it. Some of the soldiers were rude. "When you got arrested, I never got the chance to kick you." They would tell me.

"Oh no, please don't kick me." I would beg of them, "Whatever you want me to do I will do it. Just please don't kick me. You want me to wash your laundry? I will wash your laundry."

That would get me on their good side. I kept myself busy all day and night. I wouldn't rest until the commander told me that I needed to lie down and rest.

Speaking Thai became one of my best advantages. Some of the soldiers liked me because I spoke Thai. They would torture some of the other prisoners when they would not answer their questions. They did not know Thai and for that they weren't shown any favor.

As the days went on, they trusted me more and more. They eventually allowed me to walk outside the boundaries of their base and take food to the soldiers on guard duty. All of the soldiers eventually liked me because I took such good care of them.

When the month was over the commander approached me with an offer. "Do you want to stay here at our base or return to your refugee camp?"

"I want to return to the camp." I replied, "My wife could deliver the baby any day now. I want to be there."

They allowed me to return to the refugee camp. Two weeks after I returned my wife went into labor in the middle of the night. I remember asking her if she could just wait until morning to deliver because it was too dark to deliver the baby.

My second daughter, Sopheap Phang, was born November 26, 1980. She was very healthy when she was born but about a month or two later she began vomiting all the time. She eventually stopped but still suffered from stomach issues until later in her life. She was almost a year old when my name was called for an interview. I was selected to go to the United States.

FREEDOM AND FIGHTING

My family and I left Thailand in September 1981 for the United States. Our plane landed in New York City, it was so cold. When we arrived. The people at the airport handed us documents to hang around our neck, they told us never to lose them. They also gave us heavy coats to wear. Many people at the airport looked at us funny. We had flip flops on, documents hanging around our neck, and heavy coats.

We arrived in Providence, Rhode Island. My godmother's brother had arranged for Pastor Bernard Dunning and his wife, Edyth to pick my family up. They took us to an apartment that they had rented for us to stay in. Pastor Dunning and Edyth began to explain everything in the apartment.

"The lights turn on and off by flicking this switch."

"When you use the toilet, you have to flush afterwards."

"Never open the door if someone comes to knock on it, it could be dangerous."

There were so many other things that they shared with us in the little bit of time that they were there. My mind was spinning with all the instructions they told us. I began to wonder where we had gone and what we were doing here. It was so different from everything that we knew. They told us to pick up the phone and call them if there was anything that we needed and then they left.

Almost every day someone would stop by the apartment and show us how to live. They would remind us of the things we had all ready been told to do and teach us some new things like how to cook on the stove. I had a new life in the United States now but I was very homesick. The government gave us six months of support to help us transition. They provided money for rent, food, and other things. They helped us to find jobs but it wasn't easy because we did not speak English. We could not go find a job by ourselves we had to go through an agency to find a job.

Finding a job was not the only difficult thing about living in America. At that time there were a lot of people that were prejudice against Asian people because of the various wars taking place. I remember walking down the street and people yelling out "Hey Chinese, go home!" Pastor Dunning explained to us that some people acted this way because they had relatives that died in the war. They did not care if we were Chinese, Japanese, Vietnamese, or anything. All they knew was that we were Asian and so they grouped us all together for judgment. They decided that anyone that looked Asian must have been involved in the war and been a reason their relatives or friends were now dead.

Pastor Dunning told us to be patient with them. While there were small groups of people that accepted us and helped us out, there were quite a few more that rejected us and treated us horribly. They would throw cans at us and threaten us. At first, the police told us to call them if anyone ever bothered us but there became so many incidents that the police informed us not to call unless someone was hurt.

One night, we were walking back from an Independence Day celebration. When got back to our homes we realized that all the windows were broken. I told my friends that it was time to stand up to these people. We had lived through Khmer Rouge enslavement, we did not come to America to live every day in fear. We decided that the next time they bothered us we were not going to be afraid. We would fight back, and we did.

The police showed up and asked if anyone was hurt. Nobody was hurt and nobody bothered us anymore after that. Slowly, the racist people began to move off the block and new Cambodians arriving to America would occupy their homes. Eventually, the block was occupied by Cambodian people and we were living in peace. Nobody bothered us or treated us badly.

Every Sunday, Pastor Dunning would stop by and pick up my family for church. I began to know more about God. But I wasn't very happy. I still did not have a job, there was nothing for me to do. I would sleep, eat, and watch TV. I'd walk up and down the stairs several times a day because I didn't know where to go. I began writing letters to Vietnam looking for my parents and other family members. I sent many Aerograms (this was something you could send anywhere in the world) but never received a reply. I remember getting a reply about five months after sending out letters. It was a telegram with my parent's names and address. I missed them very much but had to focus on this new life in America.

My freedom was very limited because I could not understand English at all. I began to attend ESL classes at the YMCA about three miles from my house. No one had shown me how to take the bus so I would walk to school and back Monday through Friday. They eventually changed my school's location to OIC. That was much farther from my house. I had to walk to the downtown area and get on a bus that would take me to the school. After almost a year of schooling, I could speak a little bit of English. In 1981, The agency was able to find me a job with A&H MFG. CO in Johnston, RI.

Even though, I still could not speak good English, the owner liked me because of my work ethics. I was a hard worker. I worked just as hard for him as I had for the farmer, the Khmer Rouge, and the soldiers in Thailand. My work ethic had never changed. I worked hard so I could be proud of the work that I did.

About two or three months later, the owner asked me if I wanted to work overtime. He said he would pay me time and a half to work overtime. I told him that I would do this for him. He asked me how much time I wanted to work, I could work seventy to eighty hours a week if I wanted to. I ended up working eighty hours a week. I started out at $3.25 an hour and eventually was making $9.35 an hour. I saved a lot of money during that time and three years later was able to buy my own three story house for just $40,000.

Having a bigger house was greatly appreciated as my family grew with the addition of two more children. On November 3, 1983 my son Paul Tang was born. Just two years later on May 5, 1985, my second son Philip Tang was born.

My boss told me, "Lang, you are a very hard worker. If you have more friends that work hard like you I want you to bring them to me. I will hire them to work."

He hired many Cambodian and Laotian people to work for him. Word got around among the other Cambodians that they only had to know my name to get a job at my company. The manager would hire them even though they could not speak English because they worked hard.

I ran a machine that was very important to the company. It was a main part of their production and I was the only one who knew how to run it so they kept paying me more and more. My boss eventually became jealous of me because of how much money I was making. He only worked around forty hours a week where I usually worked eighty hours a week. Sometimes he would hand my paycheck to me with two hands joking that I got paid enough for two people. One day, I told him that the machine was not working right, it needed to be fixed. He ignored me and told me to keep working. The machine broke down and they had to call in a mechanic from Germany to fix it.

The mechanic couldn't figure out what was wrong with the machine. I told him everything that had happened before the machine stopped working. He found the problem and told me that I was very smart. He asked how I knew what the problem was. I showed him my Cambodian book. Every day I would write down in Cambodian everything that I needed to know. It helped me remember when things began to go wrong. It also helped me not to make any mistakes. Even though I was colorblind I would look at the numbers that every color was associated with, write it down in my Cambodian book, and have the right colors go through the machine.

They had to pay a lot of money for the Germany technician to look at the machine and I knew where the problem was. They fired my boss for not listening to me. Then they brought in a new man to be my boss. The problems began from the start. He didn't know me from anyone else in the company. He didn't understand how hard I worked and it didn't matter to him. He hired a new guy to come in and learn how to run my machine.

I did not like this guy at all. He was arrogant and prideful. I tried to teach him how to run the machine but I knew that he wasn't paying attention. When I asked him to answer questions his only response would be "piece of cake." I didn't know what "piece of cake" meant but I knew that he did not understand how to run the machine.

"You need to keep a book with notes like me." I told him and showed him my Cambodian book.

He would smile and say, "I've got this, Chinese, piece of cake. I graduated from college you know."

I didn't know what college was and it didn't matter to me. He wasn't learning how to run the machine and he wasn't very smart. No matter how many times I told him that I was Cambodian, he still called me Chinese.

A month went by and the boss asked me if the young man could run the machine. He told the boss he knew how to run it "piece of cake" but I told him that he did not know how to run the machine yet. They argued for a while and the boss told me to let him run the machine.

I let him run the machine and everything went wrong. We had to throw out so much material because he would not watch when things went off track. The boss came to us and asked what was going on. I told him that the new guy did not know how to run the machine. He asked why we never wasted materials when I was running the machine. I told him because I watched for things to go wrong and fixed them before they did. This new guy wasn't paying attention and he didn't know how to run the machine.

The boss and the new guys began to argue in English. I wasn't quite sure of everything that they were saying but I could tell that there was a lot of racist comments being said. The boss asked me again why there was a problem with production today. I told him but he wouldn't listen, he said I was a troublemaker. They called me into the office and told me that I couldn't have any more overtime because I had wasted so much material that day. I realized nothing good would come from trying to stay at this job so I punch my time card and never went back.

It was 1987. I went to the unemployment office and filled out all the paperwork to collect unemployment. They called me a week later and told me that my request had been denied because the manager told them I had quit for no reason. I told them that I had a very good reason and wanted to make an appeal. My appointment in court was schedule for 9:00AM. I went in around 8:30AM and began to tell the officer that I had a very good reason for quitting. I told him about everything that had happened to me since this new boss got hired. The officer agreed that I had a valid reason for quitting my job. The officer looked at the clock after I finished my story. It was 9:30AM and my boss still had not shown up. He asked if I knew where my boss was but I did not know. The officer told me that I won the appeal. As I was leaving the building my boss walked in. The officer told him that everything was over and I had won the appeal.

I was so happy that I had won and began collecting money. But at the same time, I wanted to know what I should do now. After two weeks, my old company called me and told me that my position was still open if I would like my job back. Nobody else was able to run the machine like I was. I told them that I was not interested in coming back at all. I don't know what they decided to do after that. I did hear later that they fired all the Cambodian and Laotians that couldn't speak English. It was probably because these people would always come to me and ask me questions if they did not understand how to do something.

Lang Tang & Nicole Donoho

THE AMERICAN DREAM

Our third son, Peter Tang, was born on September 11, 1988. We now had our hands full with five young children. We had our own home and the American dream seemed to be taking shape in our lives.

I remember my mother always told me that if I wanted to get rich I would have to work for myself. I had a lot of money and thought I should open my own grocery store. I put my house up for sale and within a week it sold for $110,000. I bought a grocery store from a friend in 1989. My store did very good because I knew most of the Cambodians living in Rhode Island at that time.

The majority of them worked for my old company. I enjoyed working at the store until the trouble began. Gangs began to harass the local businesses. One day some teenage boys came to my store and told me to give them money or they would make it miserable for me. I knew the parents of some of these boys. The boys wanted money to bail their friends out of jail. I told them that I only had enough money to live off of, there wasn't any extra money. I wasn't going to help any troublemakers. They told me that if that was the case they would take my merchandise instead.

I called the police and most of them were arrested. About three weeks later, they came back to my store. I told them that they were not allowed to shop in my store anymore. They threatened me and said, "Just wait and see what happens to you and your store."

I walked in one day and they had stolen my merchandise. They broke furniture and the front windows. I went to the police station and asked them for help. They asked what I wanted them to do. I told them that they needed to watch my store at night but they said that they could not do this all the time. I knew that I wasn't allowed to stay at the store but I asked them anyway if I could stay there overnight. I wanted to catch the men that were breaking into my store. They gave me permission to do this.

I went to a nearby gun shop and bought a .32mm with a lot of ammunition. It cost me around $265. I slept at the store for two or three nights before anything happened. It was hard to get any sleep wondering if someone would break in or not.

Then around 1:30AM I heard a noise near the front door. Two men were trying to use some tool to open the front door. The must have been with another gang because most of the time the gangs just broke the windows. I grasped my loaded gun in one hand and dialed the police with the other.

"There are some men trying to break into my store. I've got a gun but I don't want to hurt anybody." I had escaped from the killing fields. I had seen many people die during that time but I still did not want to see any more people die. Even if they were trying to rob me.

"The police are on their way. If you have to shoot anybody just make sure you shoot them as they are entering your store. Don't shoot anyone that is running away. And don't hang up, the police are on their way."

That sounded good but I didn't want to shoot anyone. Lucky for me, the police arrived within thirty seconds it seemed and surrounded the guys. I turned on the lights and the police told the thieves that they were lucky. "Do you see, he was waiting inside with a gun, you're lucky you didn't get that door open because he probably would have shot you."

A week later, a black Ram drove by the store and tried to shoot me with a shotgun. I guess they were really trying to scare me, it worked because the bullet had just barely missed me. I called the police.

About three weeks later, two big guys walked into my store. They walked up to the counter and seemed very suspicious. One of the men told the other guy to pay me for their merchandise. I noticed the guy was reaching for a gun in his coat. I grabbed his hand when he pulled the gun out and quickly smashed his hand against the counter. I pointed their .45mm at them and they ran from the store as fast as they could. I was alive once again. I called the police and told them what had happened. When they came to the store they told me that I should not have fought back. I should have gave them what they wanted and allowed the police to handle it.

That was not an option. I told the police that I had a friend who owned an Asian market on Broat Street. Some men held him up at gunpoint. He gave them everything they asked for and once they got it, they shot him in the head. I told them that I would do what I had to do to protect my life.

The officers believed my story but they didn't like it. They told me that they would do their best to patrol the area and keep an eye on me. That gave me little comfort.

About two weeks later I was at the bank and saw one of the men that held up my store. I told the police officer in charge of the bank that he was the man who had held up my store. He ran out of the bank to catch him but he was all ready gone.

I wasn't doing too well during that time. People weren't shopping at my store as much because of the robbery attempts.

They were afraid that they might get caught in the store at the wrong time. I didn't sleep or eat very well because I was worried about how I would provide for my family with business slowing down.

About two or three months later, some people broke in and destroyed almost everything in my store. I had to walk away from the store because I had no more money to repair it. It was 1996. I was now just as broke as I had been when I arrived from Thailand fifteen years earlier. I would have to start from ground zero once again.

I ONCE WAS DEAD

As far as my family was concerned, I was dead most of my life. They eventually found out that I was alive and living in America but still had their doubts.

In 1993, while I still owned my grocery store, I decided to visit my family back in Vietnam. I knew that the country was still very unstable but I felt as if it was time to see my family once again. After all, I had not seen them since 1968.

I arrived at the Phnom Penh International Airport in Cambodia. I began asking different people if they knew of my parents or the village that I needed to get to in Vietnam. Looking back, this was probably a very stupid thing to do because anyone could have kidnapped me or killed me.

I found a taxi driver that said he knew where my village was. The taxi driver warned me not to act like I was from the United States. It would be very dangerous for me if I was caught. I asked if he knew where my hometown was, so much had changed since I left years ago. He said that he was very familiar with this town. I asked if he knew the Tang family and he said yes. But he never once recognized who I was.

I got to my parents house and walked into the house. I called for my mother. She came out and cried. "I thought that you were dead." Everyone cried when they came into the house. They all thought that I had died.

My neighbor had returned from Cambodia and lived just down the street from my parents. She told them that she had not seen me since 1970 when they forced the Vietnamese in Cambodia to return to Vietnam.

My dad sat me down and told me that a boy came to him and said "Grandpa, Grandpa, Uncle Lang is home." just two days before I arrived. He thought that the boy was crazy but the next day he came to him and told him the same thing. He told the boy that he was lying but now here I was. I knew that God must have revealed to that boy I would be returning.

I only recognized my older brother and sister. Everyone else would walk up to me and say, "I'm your sister" or "I'm your brother". We all cried so much during that time. We were so excited to see each other. They were so excited to see me alive.

My dad told me that one of my brothers heard I was in America and tried to escape in 1983. They told him he would need to get into the middle of a fishing boat for the escape. Little did he know, that was the part of the boat where they stored the fish. They locked the doors and drown everyone that was trying to escape. Then they seized all his property and threw his body in the sea.

I felt as if nothing had changed over the past 25 years. It was as if I sat back down at the dinner table as a fourteen year old. My mother cooked the same food I remembered her cooking when I was young. And while we were eating she would say "Eat quickly because we don't know when there might be fighting that breaks out between Vietcong and the other soldiers."

While I was visiting, I began taking pictures of the rice fields that I worked in when I was younger. The police arrested me and told me, "This is not America. You cannot just take pictures." They argued with me and told me that they should put me in jail. They accused me of possibly being a spy. After arguing with me for a while they told me that they would forget about it if I paid them. I gave them fifty dollars and they told me I could take all the pictures I wanted.

NEW LIFE WITH A NEW WIFE

In 2000, I got divorced from my first wife. I was single once again. This meant that everyone I knew would be set on finding me a new wife. This is a very common thing in the Cambodian culture. Everyone is always trying to be a match maker.

I remember my pastor asking me if I was still single. I told him that I was and he asked what I thought of this woman named Sokha (pronounced So Car). I said that she was ok but I didn't know much about her.

After that, I found out that her pastor and my pastor began to talk about how they should get the two of us together. They did what we might consider background checks on both of us to determine whether or not we were compatible with each other. Talking with our neighbors and friends to find out what kind of things we were interested in and what kind of work we did. This is also a common practice in my culture. Then they arranged for us to meet.

After we met, we'd spend many Sunday afternoons visiting together. Sokha wanted to return to Cambodia. She missed it a lot. I told her that she should stay in the United States. I would sponsor her to get her citizenship because I was in love with her.

Two or three months went by and we decided to get married. On April 27, 2002 we got married. In 2004, her daughter and son came to live in the United States. Her son began to work hard and her daughter continued her education.

In 2005, we became the 4th place distributors in the nation for a company called Reliv and received a cruise to Mexico. It was wonderful. You can read more about the company in the "Reborn with Reliv" section of my story.

Then in 2008 we moved from Providence, Rhode Island to Northwest Arkansas. Our next door neighbor invited us to Key Point Church and we've been going there ever since. Our goal is to serve God in America, Cambodia, and Vietnam. Letting people know all that He has done for us in our lives.

Our Engagement

These pictures show our traditional Cambodian wedding outfits.

Lang Tang & Nicole Donoho

Our Wedding Day

AND LIFE GOES ON

Today, I look back on my life and see how different it is from my earlier years. I've been granted favor in times when it wasn't being given. I've continued to live when I should have died.

So many of my brothers and sisters tried to escape to America to live in freedom. They were tortured, killed, or left stranded in Cambodia. I am the only one in my family that has made it to freedom.

So many Cambodians and Vietnamese died during the war. I was shown favor, I was protected.

Reviewing my life makes me realize that nothing has been easy. But it also makes me realize how much I truly have to be grateful for. How much God has truly protected me and provided for me even when I knew nothing of his existence.

There are so many horrible things that take place in this world. Things that no one should ever live through or be a witness to. It is important not to let these things change us into something we are not. It's important that these things do not make us value life any less or give up on those around us.

I do not believe that it is by chance that you have decided to read my story. I believe it is by God's great purpose. I encourage you to ask God to become real in your life too. As I have stated throughout the story, there have been so many times I have experienced God's favor before I even knew of His existence. But after knowing Him, I have been overwhelmed by the peace and love that He freely pours out on me each new day.

I know what my mission in life is. It is to tell my story to others so that they too will find hope in their dark places. So that they too will decide to **Hold Fast** through whatever struggles they might come up against throughout their life. And that they may come to know and put their trust in the one true God.

"For God so loved the world that he gave his one and only son that whoever believes in Him shall not perish but have eternal life."
John 3:16

Lang Tang & Nicole Donoho

REBORN WITH RELIV

Although it is much different from what you have read about my earlier years of life, I decided to include this section because the information in it has had a great impact on my later years of life.

In 1997, a new chapter to my life began when a friend of mine introduced me to a company called Reliv. He told me that it had helped him in many ways. I told my friend that I would try his product out. If it worked I would tell the world.

Everyone in Providence, Rhode Island knew that I was in bad shape from the trauma I received to my back in 1973. They saw me walk around hunched over like a very old man. I took Reliv products for three months and saw a complete transformation in my health.

I began to share my story with everyone that I met. The products had changed my life and I wanted other's lives to be changed as well. Because of my own personal story and success I eventually became an ambassador for Reliv. I shared my story and others were helped as well. In 1999, I won a trip to Rome.

When I married Sokha, she had stomach problems. The doctors were very concerned because she had come to the point where she could no longer eat. She began taking Reliv products and three months later she too saw a complete transformation in her health.

Reliv has opened many doors for me. Not only was I able to tell my story about how it had changed my life but I was also able to see the health of other people changed through Reliv products. I have been able to get customers from other countries as well such as the Philippines, Canada, Mexico, Australia, New Zealand, Malaysia and various countries in Europe.

I've been taking Reliv products for over fifteen years now. I'm healthier and happier than I ever have been in my life. Many of my family and friends have begun to take them and the Reliv products have helped them in tremendous ways as well. I am so grateful to have such an impactful product as part of my life.

To find out more about Reliv products
visit their official website at:

www.reliv.com

To become a distributor you can use the following number:
RCN#259108301

Become a fan on Facebook:

www.facebook.com/holdfastbylangtang

Post reviews, find out more about Lang's story, and connect with other readers.

Behind the Scenes

This book would not have been possible if it wasn't for everyone involved. But most of all for God bringing us all together to work on such a great project.

The Instigator: Rick Stone

Even though he likes to stay in the shadows, this project came to life through the obedience to God and determination of Rick. He heard Lang's story and knew that it was something worth sharing. He soon started calling on his resources and making the whole project come to life. From the very first meeting at Lang's house on October 9, 2012 to the printed book, Rick has made sure that everyone has got where they needed to be.

The Survivors: Lang & Sokha Tang

Lang is a history book of knowledge. Everyone working on the project was amazed at his impeccable memory of the events that took place throughout his life.

Sokha made sure that we had healthy snacks for every writing session, and made sure we ate them too.

The Artist: Tim Nicholson

Tim joined the team in the last stages of the project. His amazing work on the cover truly completed the project.

He is an illustrator and digital artist who loves to create meaningful art. You can check out more of his work at timothynicholson.com. Tim lives in Arkansas with his wife and son.

The Author: Nicole Donoho

Nicole was delighted to co-author the story with Lang. It was her first biography to work on. Everyone called her the "ring leader" of the project because she kept it organized and focused.

Other work by Nicole includes a collection of self published children's books, young adult books, and a novel "Annabelle's Boots" set to re-release at the end of 2013. You can find out more about Nicole and her work by becoming a fan on Facebook (www.facebook.com/nicoledonohobooks) or by visiting her blog (http://transparencme.blogspot.com).

Made in the USA
Columbia, SC
15 May 2024